Classic Recipes of
GERMANY

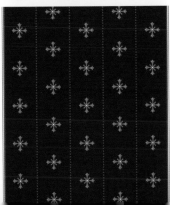

Classic Recipes of
GERMANY

TRADITIONAL FOOD AND COOKING
IN 25 AUTHENTIC DISHES

MIRKO TRENKNER

LORENZ BOOKS

This edition is published by
Lorenz Books,
an imprint of Anness Publishing Ltd,
Blaby Road, Wigston, LE18 4SE

www.lorenzbooks.com;
www.annesspublishing.com

If you like the images in this book and
would like to investigate using them for
publishing, promotions or advertising,
please visit our website
www.practicalpictures.com for more
information.

Publisher: Joanna Lorenz
Editor: Emma Clegg & Helen Sudell
Designer: Nigel Partridge
Production Controller: Steve Lang
Recipe Photography: Martin Brigdale

The image on the front cover is of Stollen
page 60

A CIP catalogue record for this book is
available from the British Library

PUBLISHER'S NOTE

Although the advice and information in this
book are believed to be accurate and true
at the time of going to press, neither the
authors nor the publisher can accept any
legal responsibility or liability for any errors
or omissions that may have been made nor
for any inaccuracies nor for any loss, harm
or injury that comes about from following
instructions or advice in this book.

PUBLISHER'S ACKNOWLEDGEMENTS

The Publisher would like to thank
iStockphoto: p5, 6, 7t, 8, 9b, 9t, 11t, 13 for
the use of their images.

COOK'S NOTES

Bracketed terms are intended for American
readers. For all recipes, quantities are given
in both metric and imperial measures and,
where appropriate, in standard cups and
spoons. Follow one set of measures, but
not a mixture, because they are not
interchangeable.

Standard spoon and cup measures are
level. 1 tsp = 5ml, 1 tbsp = 15ml, 1 cup =
250ml/8fl oz. Australian standard
tablespoons are 20ml. Australian readers
should use 3 tsp in place of 1 tbsp for
measuring small quantities.

American pints are 16fl oz/2 cups.
American readers should use 20fl oz/2.5
cups in place of 1 pint when measuring
liquids.

Electric oven temperatures in this book are
for conventional ovens. When using a fan
oven, the temperature will probably need to
be reduced by about 10–20°C/20–40°F.
Since ovens vary, you should check with
your manufacturer's instruction book for
guidance.

The nutritional analysis given for each
recipe is calculated per portion (i.e. serving
or item), unless otherwise stated. If the
recipe gives a range, such as Serves 4–6,
then the nutritional analysis will be for the
smaller portion size, i.e. 6 servings. The
analysis does not include optional
ingredients, such as salt added to taste.

Medium (US large) eggs are used unless
otherwise stated.

Contents

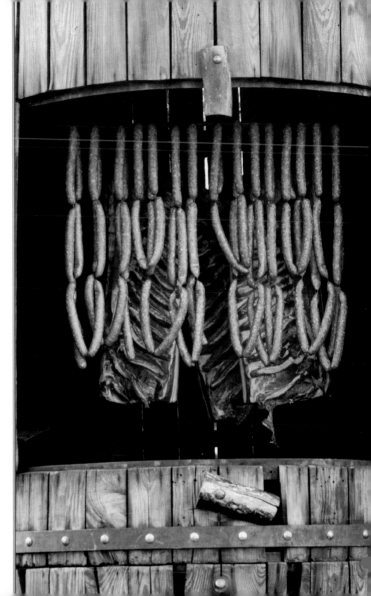

Introduction

German cuisine has its roots in the solid traditional fare of the pre-industrial age, with an abundance of dairy products, grains and vegetables from its fertile farmlands, and a passion for meat, especially in the form of the justly famous varieties of German sausage. The national cuisine is rich and varied, with notable regional distinctions between the north and south of the country, but also with many local specialities found in areas bordered by Austria, Italy and France. This book celebrates the high quality and surprising variety of German cuisine, with recipes that transform nourishing, quality ingredients into delicious traditional dishes.

Left: The russet tones of autumn vineyards in Baden, Germany's southernmost, warmest and sunniest wine-growing region.

Germany's Culinary Heritage

Germany's central position between the warm south and the cold north has ensured that its culinary influence has been felt for many hundreds of years. Even 2,000 years ago, the countryside provided pasture land for all kinds of cattle, sheep and pigs; grain and vegetables flourished in the fields; and on the warm lower slopes of the hills and mountains, hops and vines were already growing to provide the ubiquitous beer and

Below: In the autumn German families will pick wild forest mushrooms for their table.

Above: German bread is amongst the best in the world and is a staple breakfast item.

the light, refreshing wine, such as Riesling, for which Germany is rightly renowned.

Germany has many different kinds of bread, based on the various grains that can be grown, and mostly still baked using traditional methods. Rye bread, with its dark colour and rich, strong flavour, is very typical of this part of Europe. Other time-honoured recipes give us the famous German sausages, which use every part of the animal in combination with herbs and spices such as juniper berries, mustard and horseradish.

Dairy products, too, are still made in the old way, with many types of cheese, butter, yogurt, milk and soured milk products, all of which are very popular as part of the daily diet. Milk products have a key role in the German food market. There are hard cheeses made from cow's milk, as well as goat's and sheep's milk from every region of the country. As with sausages, bread and beer, every region has its own speciality and closely guarded secret recipes.

Since the 18th century, when King Frederick the Great introduced potatoes to Germany, these humble roots have become a great favourite – many delicious recipes for soups, salads and pancakes feature potato as a main ingredient. Other vegetables such as onions and cabbage are just as important to the German cook, most notably in the national dish sauerkraut.

Right: Rich and comforting, a hearty casserole is a favourite country meal.

German Food Traditions

Eating in Germany has always focused on cooking fresh wholesome food for the family meal, and recently home cooking has become more international with Germans happily adopting ingredients and dishes from other countries. In rural areas, however, the traditional cuisine still dominates, and the best of the age-old recipes and methods are maintained with great pride.

Culinary map of Germany

Germany is divided into 16 federal states: ten in the western part of the country and six in the

Below: Pretzels are popular pastries with all Germans.

east. These states are quite varied in their landscape, climate and history.

In the north, busy ports such as Hamburg have a cosmopolitan feel, with an international influence on the local cuisine that was established many years ago. Bremen, Hamburg, Lübeck, and Rostock are ancient Hanseatic cities, part of a trading group that dominated the Baltic and North Sea for 400 years. Merchants in these ports dealt in goods from all over the world, including exotic spices, rice, coffee and tea, and this meant that the daily food of people in the northern states was not only based on local produce, but was also enriched by all kinds of exciting tastes from abroad. Another influence on the northern cuisine is the coastline, which means there is a wide range of seafood on the menu.

The central part of Germany (Brandenburg, North Rhine Westphalia, Saxony-Anhalt, Saxony, Thuringia and Hesse) is

Above: A wine-producing village on the river Mosel.

home to a very rustic, natural cuisine based on fresh, locally grown staples as well as some more recent imports. Saxony is the place to find the best cakes, gateaux, pastries and a coffee culture with a long tradition.

Berlin, in the north-east, is a city state, the most international town in Germany. As far back as the 17th century, Huguenot refugees from France brought their own ideas of cooking to the area. Today, influences from all over the world create a delicious fusion cuisine in Berlin, with its roots still firmly in German traditions.

The south, made up of the states of Rhineland Palatinate, Baden-Württemberg, Saarland and Bavaria, has the most distinguished regional cuisine. The influence of the bordering countries, France, Switzerland and Austria, brought an interest in the best techniques and finest ingredients. The Bavarians particularly love pork in all its forms – roasted, in stews and soups, and preserved as whole hams and many different types of sausage. With its long hot summers the climate is ideal for vines, and this is the best wine-producing area in Germany.

Below: Barbecued sausages are essential fare at any celebration.

Food throughout the day

Breakfast is an important meal, with a range of different breads, jam, cheese, ham, eggs and sausages. The main meal of the day used to be lunch, when hot soups, stews and other main courses based on meat or fish were served plus a dessert; later in the day, dinner would be a cold meal, with bread, salad and again cheese, sausages and ham. These days the meals are often reversed, with a cold lunch and a hot evening meal.

Above: Gingerbread hearts for sale at the Oktoberfest market.

For special occasions, the deeply routed traditions of German cuisine are evident. When families come together for a feast the highlight is always a time-honoured dish such as lamb at Easter, and goose or duck at Christmas, almost always accompanied by pork knuckle, sauerkraut, stollen and gingerbread, washed down with a fine Riesling or Mosel wine.

Classic Ingredients

German cooks like to choose local produce in season, harking back to the times when country life was dominated by whatever was available in the vegetable plot, ripe in the fields and hedgerows or had been stored in the larder.

Fish

German recipes often use fresh sea fish such as cod, herring and salmon, caught in the cold waters of the North Sea and the Baltic off the northern coast. Herring dishes abound, while Alaskan pollack (coalfish) and tuna are becoming very popular.

Below: Herring is a popular and versatile ingredient.

Produce from the many rivers and lakes of Germany features less often than sea fish. One exception is the delicious trout from the fast-flowing streams of the central region. Whole carp and pike are still roasted on special occasions, particularly on Good Friday.

Smoking is one of the oldest methods of preserving fish, and gives it a unique flavour. Smoked eel and herring seem to have a particular affinity with Germany's strong-tasting dark rye bread, and make a favourite snack or light lunch.

Meat

Every part of the pig is used in German recipes, not just the best cuts. Pork knuckle is a traditional dish that makes the most of a lesser cut by braising it very slowly until it is mouthwateringly tender.

German sausages are nearly all based on pork, with the addition of any amount of different herbs, vegetables, grains and spices; it is said that there are at least 1,500 varieties.

Above: Slices of ham appear on many German breakfast tables.

They are eaten on their own (fried, grilled (broiled) or poached), with bread, or added to soups and stews.

Another preserved meat is smoked, dried or cooked ham. Black Forest ham is a typical example of the delicious regional variations still available in Germany, some of which can take months to prepare properly. Beef, lamb and venison are all part of German culinary history but tend to be reserved for special occasions.

Right: Smoking fish is an age old tradition in Germany.

Above: German cheeses are renowned throughout the world.

Poultry and Game

Chicken is still popular throughout Germany and is another convenient source of protein found on the family farm. Venison, hare, duck and goose

Below: Fresh fruit is a key ingredient in many desserts.

are all part of German culinary history and they tend to be cooked as the centrepiece of a special meal such as Easter Sunday lunch or a family birthday celebration.

Dairy Products

Many different kinds of cheese play a central role in German meals, for example, strong tasty cheese is an important ingredient in the famous Bavarian snack, Brotzeit, a delicious mixture of cheese, ham and gherkins on full-bodied dark rye bread,

The lush pasture lands of southern Germany are ideal grazing grounds, giving quantities of creamy milk. Sour cream is stirred into soups, and makes a topping for pancakes. Dairy products are also used as a base for many fruit desserts.

Fruit

The favourite locally-grown fruit in Germany is the apple, as apples are available over most of the year. The start of summer brings the berry season, when

strawberries are soon followed by raspberries, blueberries, blackberries, red and black currants. Rumtopf, a compote of preserved fruit in alcohol, makes the most of seasonal fruits, resulting in a heady concoction for the cold and dark of the winter months.

Vegetables

Germans are particularly fond of potatoes. They fry, boil and mash them, eat them cold in salad, and form them into dumplings and pancakes.

The brassica season lasts the whole year, so these vegetables have always been

Below: White asparagus is a German delicacy.

Above: Red cabbage is added to soups, stews and salads.

Above: Pumpkin soup is a favourite autumn dish.

staple foods in Germany. White and red cabbage, Brussels sprouts, cauliflower, curly kale, kohlrabi, Savoy cabbage and pointed cabbage are widely used raw, cooked or fried; these vegetables are real all-rounders. They crop up in many German recipes, for example in soups, added to meat or game stew, stuffed and rolled with minced (ground) meat, and thinly sliced as part of a cold salad.

In late spring, Germans enjoy both white and green asparagus as a side dish or as the basis for a delicate appetizer, served with smoked fish and a creamy piquant dressing.

There are lots of other vegetables that Germans enjoy. Beetroot (beet) is a special favourite, as are carrots and, in the autumn, squashes such as pumpkin. Germans also enjoy hunting for wild mushrooms from late summer through the autumn months. Chanterelles are the most common variety, but the woods are also full of porcini and morels.

Flavourings and Condiments
German dishes are rarely hot and spicy. Popular herbs are parsley, thyme, laurel, and chives, while the most common spices are black pepper (used in small amounts), juniper berries and caraway. Caraway imparts a warm, gentle flavour and is used in sauerkraut, stews, breads and cheeses. Cardamom, aniseed and cinnamon are used in cakes or beverages associated with Christmas, and sometimes in the preparation of sausages.

When it comes to condiments, mustard is the German favourite, especially with the beloved sausage. Horseradish is also commonly used. Gherkins are very popular, particularly served with cheese.

Below: Traditional spices, such as caraway, are added to many cakes and sweet pastries, particularly at Christmas.

Recipes from the Old Country

Traditional German food is steeped in the history of its rich and varied landscape, with an abundance of products from its fertile farmlands and well-stocked rivers. The classic hearty ingredients, such as sauerkraut, pork knuckle, rye wheat and beer, still feature prominently in many German homes and restaurants. The recipes that follow honour this heritage in a collection of authentic starters and salads, tempting light meals, rich fish and meat dishes, and delectable desserts, puddings, cakes and pastries.

Left: From an early age children are taught to bake by their grandmothers.

Parsnip Soup with Black Forest Ham
Pastinakensuppe

Serves 4

50g/2oz/4 tbsp butter
1 onion, chopped
1 garlic clove, chopped
400g/14oz parsnips, peeled and cut
   into chunks
100ml/3½fl oz/½ cup apple juice
pinch of freshly grated nutmeg
500ml/17fl oz/generous 2 cups
   chicken stock
100ml/3½fl oz/scant ½ cup single
   (light) cream
100ml/3½fl oz/scant ½ cup sour
   cream
15ml/1 tbsp sunflower oil
12 slices Black Forest ham, cut into
   fine strips
salt and ground white pepper
chopped parsley, to garnish

*Before the potato
conquered German cuisine
in the 18th century, the
parsnip was the most
common vegetable, and its
distinctive sweet flavour is
still very popular.*

1 Melt the butter in a large pan over medium heat. Gently fry the onion and garlic for about 3 minutes, until softened. Add the parsnips and stir in the apple juice. Season with salt, white pepper and nutmeg and add the stock. Bring to the boil, turn down the heat and simmer for 20 minutes, until the parsnips are soft.

2 Blend until smooth using a hand blender or in a food processor. Stir in both the cream and sour cream and return to the boil.

3 Heat the oil in a frying pan over high heat and fry the strips of ham until they are crisp. Pour the soup into hot bowls and sprinkle with ham and chopped parsley.

Carrot and Apple Cream Soup
Karotten-Apfelcreme

Serves 4

50g/2oz/4 tbsp butter
1 onion, roughly chopped
1 garlic clove, roughly chopped
500g/1¼lb carrots, roughly chopped
1 large apple, peeled, cored and
    roughly chopped
100ml/3½fl oz/scant ½ cup Riesling
500ml/17fl oz/generous 2 cups
    vegetable stock
100ml/3½fl oz/scant ½ cup apple
    juice
200ml/7fl oz/scant 1 cup single
    (light) cream
100ml/3½fl oz/scant ½ cup crème
    fraîche
15ml/1 tbsp pumpkin seeds and
    5ml/1 tsp snipped fresh chives, to
    garnish
salt and ground white pepper

*Combining the sweetness of
carrots with the fruity taste
of apples creates a
wonderful soup that you can
enjoy at any time of year.*

1 Melt the butter in a pan over medium heat. Add the onion and cook for 5 minutes until softened. Add the garlic and cook for a few minutes more. Stir in the carrots and the apples.

2 Add the Riesling, followed by the stock and the apple juice. Season with salt and white pepper. Bring to the boil, reduce the heat and simmer for 15 minutes.

3 Add the cream and the crème fraîche and bring the soup to the boil again. Blend the soup with a hand blender. If it seems too thick, add some more stock.

4 Heat a frying pan and gently dry-fry the pumpkin seeds for 3 minutes, until toasted, stirring occasionally. Sprinkle with salt. When serving the soup, sprinkle some pumpkin seeds on top and scatter with chives.

Asparagus and Smoked Fish Salad
Spargelsalat mit geräuchertem Fisch

Serves 4

600g/1lb 6oz white asparagus, peeled and cut diagonally into 1cm/½in pieces
300g/11oz green asparagus, peeled and sliced as above
20ml/4 tsp sunflower oil
1 onion, finely sliced
15ml/1 tbsp cider vinegar
15ml/1 tbsp apple juice
10 cherry tomatoes, halved
finely chopped parsley
400g/14oz mixed smoked fish (salmon, trout, eel, mackerel or halibut)
salt, ground white pepper, sugar

For the sauce

200ml/7fl oz/scant 1 cup yogurt
200ml/7fl oz/scant 1 cup sour cream
5ml/1 tsp medium-hot mustard
juice of ½ lemon
2 hard-boiled eggs, separated into yolk and white
10ml/2 tsp sunflower oil
150g/5oz fresh herbs (chervil, parsley, chives, watercress, sorrel, borage and salad burnet), very finely chopped
salt, ground white pepper, sugar

1 Cook the prepared asparagus in separate pans in salted water for 4–5 minutes or until just tender. Drain and refresh under cold running water. The stems should retain a little bite. Put the white asparagus in a bowl and set the green aside.

2 Heat the oil in a frying pan over medium heat and cook the onion for 2 minutes until slightly softened. Then add the vinegar and apple juice and season with salt, pepper and sugar. Bring the mixture to the boil and remove from the heat. Pour the hot dressing over the white asparagus. Stir in the cherry tomatoes and leave the salad to marinate for 1–2 hours.

3 To make the Frankfurt green sauce, mix the yogurt with the sour cream, mustard and lemon juice and season to taste with salt, white pepper and sugar.

4 Mash the egg yolk with a fork and blend with the oil, then stir into the yogurt and cream mixture. Finely dice the cooked egg white and mix into the dressing, together with the chopped herbs.

5 Drain the white asparagus and tomatoes from the dressing and toss with the green asparagus and the chopped parsley. Arrange the salad on serving plates, surrounded by the sliced or flaked smoked fish. Serve the sauce on the side.

This colourful salad with an intense flavour is accompanied by Frankfurt green sauce, which is served with many dishes involving fish or pan-fried meat. The classic recipe includes seven different fresh herbs, but if you can't find them all just use larger quantities of the ones you have.

Tartare of Matjes Herring and Salmon
Matjestartar auf Pumpernickel

1 Wash the herring fillets under cold running water, pat dry with kitchen paper, then with a sharp knife, cut into small cubes. Place the cut fillets in a large bowl.

2 Stir the diced apple and onion into the herring. Add the lemon juice and chives and season with ground white pepper.

3 Cut the salmon fillet into cubes the same size as the herring and place in a separate bowl. Add the red onion and mix together, then add the oil, lemon juice and sour cream. Season with salt and ground white pepper. Stir in the dill.

4 Butter the pumpernickel slices and cut them in half diagonally. Divide the herring tartare among half of the pieces and the salmon tartare among the remainder.

5 Garnish with snipped chives or a sprig of dill and serve on a board. Alternatively, arrange some salad leaves on individual plates and top with the bread slices.

Matjes, or soused, herring is very popular in Germany, especially in the north. It is always eaten cold, sometimes in conjunction with hot side dishes. This appetizer is a combination of two tartares, totally different in character: the herring is strong and salty, while the salmon has a fine, fresh flavour. Traditional Westphalian pumpernickel is a dark, slightly sweet bread made of shredded rye grains soaked in water and then baked extremely slowly. It keeps for a long time and is one of the most typically German breads.

Serves 4

For the herring tartare
200g/7oz matjes herring fillets
1 small apple, peeled and finely diced
1 small onion, finely diced
juice of ½ lemon
15ml/1 tbsp snipped fresh chives
ground white pepper

For the salmon tartare
200g/7oz skinless, boneless salmon fillet
1 small red onion, finely diced
15ml/1 tbsp sunflower oil
juice of ½ lemon
20ml/4 tsp sour cream
15ml/1 tbsp chopped fresh dill
salt and ground white pepper

To serve
8–10 slices pumpernickel
butter, for spreading
snipped chives and dill sprigs, to garnish

Potato Salad with Frankfurters
Pellkartoffelsalat mit Frankfurter Würstchen

Serves 4

750g/1¾lb waxy potatoes
5ml/1 tsp caraway seeds
3 bay leaves
15ml/1 tbsp sunflower oil
2 white onions, finely diced
100g/3½oz bacon, diced
15ml/1 tbsp white wine vinegar
250ml/8fl oz/1 cup chicken stock
small bunch fresh parsley and small
    bunch fresh chives, finely chopped
1 cucumber, peeled and halved
    lengthways, seeds removed, sliced
8 frankfurters
salt, ground white pepper and sugar
medium-hot mustard, to serve

Potato salad is a classic dish in every region of Germany. There are many different ways to prepare it, and this is a lighter version without mayonnaise. It tastes best when freshly made and eaten at room temperature.

1 Put the unpeeled potatoes in a pan with the caraway seeds and bay leaves. Boil in salted water until tender. Remove from the heat, drain and leave to cool. When cool enough to handle, peel and slice the potatoes and place in a bowl.

2 Heat the oil in a frying pan over medium heat and sweat the diced onion and bacon. Add the vinegar and chicken stock and season with salt, pepper and sugar. Bring to the boil, remove from the heat and stir the mixture into the potato. Add the herbs and sliced cucumber to the bowl. Set aside for the flavours to blend.

3 Put the frankfurters in a pan with cold water to cover and heat gently. Simmer for 8–10 minutes until heated through. Don't allow the water to boil or the frankfurters will burst. Serve with the potato salad and German mustard.

Red Cabbage Salad with Walnuts
Rotkohlsalat mit Wallnüssen

Serves 4

800g/1¾lb red cabbage
30ml/2 tbsp red wine vinegar
10ml/2 tsp sunflower oil
75g/3oz shelled walnuts
20ml/4 tsp apple sauce
5ml/1 tsp cranberry jelly
salt, ground white pepper and sugar

1 Trim the red cabbage and slice it finely. Put it in a bowl, season with salt, pepper and sugar, and pour over the vinegar and sunflower oil. Toss the salad thoroughly, using your hands, then place in the refrigerator and chill for at least 3 hours to allow the cabbage to absorb the dressing.

2 Just before serving, heat a frying pan over medium heat and toast the shelled walnuts gently, stirring, for 3–4 minutes, until lightly browned and fragrant.

3 Mix the apple sauce and the cranberry jelly, and stir into the cabbage salad. Taste the cabbage and add extra salt, vinegar or sugar as necessary. Turn into a salad bowl and scatter with the toasted walnuts.

A fresh, crunchy salad of raw red cabbage is rich in vitamins and minerals and is particularly good in winter, when fresh vegetables are more limited. You can make the salad with white cabbage too, but use white wine vinegar for the dressing. This is delicious served with slices of smoked duck breast.

Serves 4

500g/1¼lb plain (all-purpose) flour
6 eggs, lightly beaten
250ml/8fl oz/1 cup lukewarm water
20ml/4 tsp sunflower oil
pinch of freshly grated nutmeg
25g/1oz/2 tbsp butter
250g/9oz/2¼ cups grated
  Emmental cheese
2 onions, thinly sliced
salt and ground white pepper

For the salad

1 lettuce
150ml/¼ pint/⅔ cup natural (plain)
  yogurt
juice of ½ lemon
15ml/1 tbsp snipped chives
pinch of sugar
100g/3½oz cherry tomatoes, halved,
  to garnish
salt and ground white pepper

Spätzle with Cheese and Onions Kässpätzle

1 Preheat the oven to 200°C/400°F/Gas 6. Put the flour in a bowl and make a well in the centre. Add the eggs, water, 5ml/1 tsp oil and nutmeg, and beat to make a firm dough. Continue beating for 2–3 minutes until bubbles start to rise.

2 Bring a large pan of salted water to the boil. Put the dough into a potato ricer and, holding it over the pan, push carefully until strips of dough start to emerge and fall into the water. When the spätzle float to the surface they are done. Remove them with a slotted spoon and transfer to a bowl of cold water, then drain.

3 Butter a baking tray and spread a layer of spätzle over the base. Cover with a layer of grated cheese, then spätzle and repeat, ending with a layer of cheese. Bake for 7–10 minutes until the cheese is melted and lightly browned.

4 Meanwhile, heat the rest of the oil in a pan and fry the onions, stirring occasionally, until browned. Scatter them over the baked spätzle.

5 Put the lettuce in a bowl. Mix the yogurt with the lemon juice and chives and season to taste with salt, pepper and sugar. Pour the dressing over the lettuce, garnish with the tomatoes and serve with the spätzle.

Spätzle is the German form of pasta from Swabia, a region of southern Germany. It's important to get the consistency of the dough right and to beat some air into it: you'll see bubbles coming up when it's ready. Traditionally, the dough is smoothed out thinly on a wooden board using the hands and then chopped into thin strips with a knife, but it's easier to use a potato ricer.

Potato Pancakes with Smoked Salmon
Reibekuchen mit Lachs aus dem Rauch

1 To make the pancakes, mix the potato, onion, flour and eggs together and season with nutmeg, salt and pepper. Heat some oil in a frying pan over high heat.

2 Drop spoonfuls of the mixture into the pan to form small pancakes, about 6cm/2½in in diameter and 1cm/½in thick, and fry for 2–3 minutes on each side. Remove and drain on kitchen paper while you cook the rest of the pancakes.

3 Mix the sour cream with the lemon juice and the chopped herbs, and season with salt, pepper and a pinch of sugar.

4 Arrange the pancakes on a serving plate with the smoked salmon and garnish with salad leaves. Spoon some of the sour cream dressing over and serve the rest separately.

Serves 4

For the pancakes
1.5kg/3lb potatoes, peeled and
   finely grated
3 onions, finely chopped
10ml/2 tsp plain (all-purpose) flour
3 eggs
pinch of freshly grated nutmeg
sunflower oil, for frying
salt and ground white pepper

For the sour cream dressing
250ml/8fl oz/1 cup sour cream
juice of ½ lemon
handful each of fresh parsley, chives
   and dill, finely chopped
pinch of sugar
salt and ground white pepper

To serve
12 slices smoked salmon
salad leaves, to garnish

Potato pancakes are very easy to make and can be served in many different ways, both savoury and sweet. Here, they are partnered with smoked salmon and a cool sour cream dressing with fresh herbs, but you can use any other smoked fish you prefer, or try them for breakfast with fried eggs.

Nuremberg Sausages with Apple Sauerkraut
Nürnberger Rostbratwürste auf Apfelsauerkraut

Serves 4

25g/1oz butter
50g/2oz bacon, diced
1 onion, chopped
500g/1¼lb canned sauerkraut
3 allspice berries
3 bay leaves
2.5ml/½ tsp caraway seeds
200ml/7fl oz/scant 1 cup apple juice
1 apple, peeled, cored and diced
2 carrots, grated
5ml/1 tsp potato flour (potato starch)
30ml/2 tbsp oil
24 Nuremberg sausages
salt, ground white pepper and sugar
chopped parsley, to garnish
medium-hot mustard and
    pumpernickel bread, to serve

1 Heat the butter in a large pan over medium heat and gently fry the bacon and onion for about 3 minutes. Add the sauerkraut, allspice, bay leaves, caraway seeds and apple juice. Cook for 30 minutes, stirring occasionally and adding more apple juice if needed. Add the apple cubes and grated carrots and cook for a further 5 minutes.

2 Blend the potato flour to a smooth paste with a little apple juice or water and stir it into the sauerkraut. As it comes back to the boil, the remaining juices will thicken and the sauerkraut will become shiny. Season to taste with salt, pepper and sugar, then spoon into a serving dish and keep warm.

3 Heat the oil in a frying pan over high heat, and fry the sausages for 6–10 minutes, turning frequently, until they are browned on all sides and cooked through. Arrange the cooked sausages on top of the sauerkraut and garnish with chopped parsley. Serve with mustard and slices of pumpernickel bread.

These little sausages are among Germany's finest. Only as long as your finger, they should weigh no more than 25–30g/1oz apiece. Restaurants offer them in portions of a dozen or half dozen, and they make a perfect snack with sauerkraut and beer. If you cannot source Nuremberg sausages, other thin spicy sausages will do just as well.
Guten Appetit und Prost!

Apple and Potato Mash with Black Pudding
Himmel und Erde mit Gebratener Blutwurst

Serves 4

500g/1¼lb floury potatoes, boiled
45ml/3 tbsp oil
2 onions, chopped
500g/1¼lb apples, peeled and diced
juice of 1 lemon
5ml/1 tsp sugar
100g/3½oz/7 tbsp butter
100g/3½oz bacon
500g/1¼lb black pudding (blood
   sausage)
pinch of freshly grated nutmeg
salt and ground white pepper
15ml/1 tbsp chopped parsley, to
   garnish

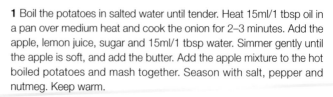

1 Boil the potatoes in salted water until tender. Heat 15ml/1 tbsp oil in a pan over medium heat and cook the onion for 2–3 minutes. Add the apple, lemon juice, sugar and 15ml/1 tbsp water. Simmer gently until the apple is soft, and add the butter. Add the apple mixture to the hot boiled potatoes and mash together. Season with salt, pepper and nutmeg. Keep warm.

2 Heat the remaining oil in two frying pans over high heat. Fry the bacon cubes in one for 4–5 minutes until crisp and browned. Take out and keep warm. Slice the black pudding and fry the slices until browned on both sides.

3 Spoon the apple and potato mash on to four plates, then put the fried black pudding on top and sprinkle some bacon cubes over it. Garnish with chopped parsley.

VARIATION

If you don't like black pudding, replace it with mini burgers made from minced (ground) pork, or some sliced spicy sausages.

In German this dish is known as 'heaven and earth'– heaven for the apple, and earth for the potato. The recipe comes from Westphalia in the middle of Germany, and is a winning combination of fruity and savoury ingredients.

Matjes Herring with Bacon and Onions
Matjesfilet mit Speckstippe

1 Boil the potatoes in salted water until tender. Meanwhile, cook the trimmed beans in boiling salted water for 6–8 minutes, then drain and refresh under cold running water. They should still be crisp with a fresh green colour.

2 Heat the butter in a pan over medium heat and fry the bacon in it for about 3 minutes, then add the chopped onion. Cook for a further minute, then add the cooked beans. Season with salt and pepper and stir in the chopped savory.

3 Drain the potatoes and arrange on a serving plate with the herring fillets and the beans. Garnish with onion rings.

COOK'S TIP
If you can't find savory, use some fresh thyme instead. Sauce remoulade, or tartare sauce, makes a good accompaniment for this dish.

Serves 4
1kg/2¼lb potatoes, peeled
1kg/2¼lb green beans, trimmed
100g/3½oz butter
200g/7oz bacon, diced
3 onions, 2 chopped and 1 sliced into
    fine rings
15ml/1 tbsp chopped fresh savory
8 matjes herring fillets
salt and ground white pepper

Formerly a fish for the poor man's table, nowadays matjes herring is a delicacy. It is a young fish, caught in the Atlantic during May and June, and is very tender, with pink flesh and a silvery skin. If you find the salty taste too strong, soak the fillets in milk for a couple of hours before cooking for a milder flavour.

Fish Fillets in Creamy Mustard Sauce
Hamburger Pannfisch mit Senfsauce

Serves 4

300ml/½ pint/1¼ cups fish stock
100ml/3½oz/scant ½ cup single
   (light) cream
10ml/2 tsp grainy mustard
sunflower oil, for frying
1kg/2¼lb boiled potatoes, thinly
   sliced
150g/5oz bacon, diced into cubes
1 onion, finely chopped
small bunch chives, chopped
800g/1¾lb fish fillets (cod, salmon,
   trout, pike or perch)
juice of 1 lemon
salt and ground white pepper
fresh dill, to garnish

1 Heat the fish stock and season it, if necessary, with salt and white pepper. Add the cream and mustard and simmer for 5 minutes to make the sauce.

2 Heat some oil in a frying pan over high heat and fry the potato slices and the bacon until browned and crisp. Add the onion and fry for another 5 minutes. Season with salt and pepper and stir in the chives.

3 Meanwhile, season the fish with lemon juice, salt and pepper. Heat some oil in another pan and fry the fillets, turning once, until golden on both sides. Arrange the fried potatoes in the middle of a serving plate with the fish round them and pour the sauce around. Garnish with chopped fresh dill.

COOK'S TIP
If the sauce seems too thin, thicken it with about 5ml/1 tsp cornflour (cornstarch) slaked in a little cold water.

This dish from northern Germany is one of my all-time favourite meals. You can use any kind of fish that is good for pan-frying, or a mix of different kinds. The mustard sauce is made with grainy mustard to add texture to the dish. Fried potatoes with bacon and onions are a perfect accompaniment.

Rhenish Mussels with Root Vegetables
Rheinische Muscheln mit Wurzelgemüse

Serves 4

4 medium carrots
2 large sticks celery
2 medium onions
2 garlic cloves
15ml/1 tbsp sunflower oil
2kg/4½lb mussels, cleaned
300ml/½ pint/1¼ cups Riesling, or
    other dry white wine
2 sprigs parsley
2 sprigs thyme
2 bay leaves
salt and ground white pepper
chopped parsley, to garnish
white bread, to serve

1 Peel all the vegetables. Cut the carrot and celery into fine matchsticks or dice, and thinly slice the onions. Peel and finely chop the garlic.

2 Heat the oil in a large pan over high heat. Add the mussels, the prepared vegetables and the garlic. Stir well and add the white wine and the herbs. Season with salt and pepper.

3 Cover the pan tightly and leave the mussels to cook for about 5 minutes, until the shells have opened. Discard any mussels that remain closed. Spoon into bowls and sprinkle with chopped parsley. Serve with fresh white bread.

COOK'S TIP
Do not cook any mussels that have broken shells, or are open and do not close when sharply tapped.

In Northern Europe, mussels are at their plumpest and best in the cooler months of the year – from September to April. In this simple dish the delicious juices from the mussels combine with the Riesling to make a wonderful sauce.

Simmered Beef Topside with Horseradish
Gesottener Tafelspitz mit Meerrettichsauce

1 Put the beef in a pan with cold water to cover, bring to the boil and skim off any scum. Reduce the heat and leave the meat to simmer for about 45 minutes. Add the chopped vegetables, spices and parsley stalks to the pan and continue to cook for about 1½ hours, until the beef is tender. Lift out the beef and keep it warm. Season the stock with salt to taste and reserve.

2 Put the sliced vegetables in a pan with 1 litre/1¾ pints/4 cups of the beef stock, bring to the boil, lower the heat and simmer until the vegetables are tender. Season with salt and, if the stock is not rich enough, part or all of a beef stock cube.

3 Melt the butter in a pan over medium heat and stir in the flour. Gradually add 500ml/17fl oz/generous 2 cups of the beef stock, stirring. Bring it to the boil and add the creamed horseradish, lemon juice and cream.

4 Stir the chopped parsley into the vegetables and stock, and spoon on to serving plates. Slice the beef and arrange it on top. Serve the sauce separately.

This dish originally came from Austria but has been very popular in Germany for a long time. Slowly simmering the meat provides a delicious stock, which you then use to cook the accompanying vegetables.

Serves 4
1kg/2¼lb beef topside
2 medium carrots, chopped
100g/3½oz celeriac, chopped
½ leek, trimmed, cleaned and chopped
2 onions, halved
3 bay leaves
4 allspice berries
5 black peppercorns
a few parsley stalks

For the accompanying vegetables
1 parsnip, sliced
4 medium carrots, sliced
2–3 sticks celery, sliced
1 large potato, peeled and sliced
200g/7oz swede (rutabaga), peeled and sliced
beef stock cube (optional)

For the sauce
30ml/2 tbsp butter
30ml/2 tbsp plain (all-purpose) flour
45ml/3 tbsp creamed horseradish
juice of 1 lemon
200ml/7fl oz/scant 1 cup single (light) cream
30ml/2 tbsp chopped parsley
salt

Veal Meatballs in White Caper Sauce
Königsberger Klopse mit Kapernsauce

Serves 4

2 day-old white bread rolls, about
100g/3½oz total weight
1kg/2¼lb minced (ground) veal
2 onions, finely chopped
2 anchovies, finely chopped
10ml/2 tsp capers
15ml/1 tbsp chopped parsley
5ml/1 tsp medium-hot mustard
2 eggs
200ml/7fl oz/scant 1 cup single
(light) cream
50g/2oz/4 tbsp butter
50g/2oz/½ cup plain (all-purpose)
flour
salt and ground white pepper
boiled rice, to serve

1 Soak the bread rolls in water, then squeeze them out, break into small pieces and place in a mixing bowl. Add the veal, onion and anchovies. Chop half the capers and add them to the bowl, with 5ml/1 tsp of the parsley and the mustard. Season, then add the eggs and mix thoroughly. Form into 12–14 meatballs.

2 Bring a pan of salted water to the boil over high heat and add the meatballs. Reduce the heat and leave to simmer for 8–10 minutes. Remove the meatballs with a slotted spoon, reserving the stock, and keep them warm in a low oven.

3 Transfer 500ml/17fl oz/generous 2 cups of the cooking water to a pan and bring it to the boil. Stir in the cream. Knead the butter with the flour to make a beurre manié (see cook's tip) and stir the mixture, a little at a time, into the boiling sauce until it is thickened.

4 Add the remaining capers and let the sauce cook for 3 minutes, then put the meatballs back into it. Garnish with the remaining chopped parsley and serve with rice.

COOK'S TIP

A beurre manié (or kneaded butter) is a paste of butter and flour, added in small pieces to a sauce at the end of cooking. It gives a smooth rich consistency.

*This dish comes from Königsberg, a medieval Baltic port.
The mild, creamy sauce complements the veal very well.
I think the capers give it a special character but if you
don't like them, they can be omitted.*

Cabbage Stuffed with Pork
Kohlrouladen mit Speckstreifen

1 Soak the bread rolls in water, then squeeze them out and break into small pieces. Put the pieces into a large mixing bowl. Add the pork, eggs and mustard and season with salt, pepper, caraway and paprika. Use your hands to mix well.

2 Trim the base from the cabbage leaves. Blanch in boiling salted water for 6 minutes, then drain and refresh under cold running water. Dry the leaves thoroughly.

3 Place a spoonful of the meat filling in the lower centre of each cabbage leaf. Flip the sides of the leaf over the filling and roll it up. Secure the end with a cocktail stick (toothpick).

4 Preheat the oven to 160°C/325°F/Gas 3. Heat a little oil in a frying pan over high heat and fry the cabbage rolls for 2 minutes on each side. As they are done, take them out and place them in a baking dish.

5 Add the onion and bacon to the pan and fry for 2 minutes, then add the stock. Bring to the boil and pour the contents of the pan over the cabbage rolls. Bake for about 15 minutes. Garnish with chopped parsley and serve with mashed potatoes.

Serves 4

2 day-old white bread rolls, about
   100g/3½oz total weight
800g/1¾lb minced (ground) pork
2 eggs
5ml/1 tsp medium-hot mustard
pinch of ground caraway seeds
pinch of paprika
8 large leaves from a white cabbage
oil for frying
2 onions, chopped
200g/7oz smoked bacon, diced
200ml/7fl oz/scant 1 cup chicken
   stock
salt and ground white pepper
chopped parsley, to garnish
mashed potatoes, to serve

This dish reminds me of my mother. I really loved her cooking, especially her Kohlrouladen. This way of stuffing cabbage leaves is popular all over Germany, though the spices used vary slightly from region to region.

Chicken in Riesling with Roast Potatoes
Hühnchen in Riesling mit Kleinen Röstkartoffeln

1 Preheat the oven to 180°C/350°F/Gas 4. Heat 15ml/1 tbsp of the oil in a large flameproof casserole over high heat. Season the chicken joints generously and fry them on all sides until the skin is golden brown and crisp. Add the white wine, bring to the boil and transfer the dish to the preheated oven. Cook for 30 minutes.

2 Meanwhile, put the potatoes in a baking tray, season with salt and pepper and toss in the remaining oil. Put the tray in the oven and roast for 30–40 minutes.

3 Take the chicken out of the oven, remove the joints and keep them warm. Over a medium heat, cook the onions, garlic and mushrooms in juices from the chicken and the reduced wine, then add the cream and bring back to the boil. Season well.

4 Arrange one chicken leg and one breast on warmed plates. Pour over some sauce and mushrooms and garnish with chopped parsley. Serve with the roast potatoes.

VARIATION
This dish is just as delicious when served with fresh noodles rather than roast potatoes.

Serves 4

45ml/3 tbsp sunflower oil
4 chicken legs
4 chicken breasts
250ml/8fl oz/1 cup Riesling or other
    dry German white wine
800g/1¾lb small potatoes, halved
2 onions, thinly sliced
1 garlic clove, finely chopped
200g/7oz brown cap (cremini)
    mushrooms, sliced
500ml/17 fl oz/2 cups single (light)
    cream
salt and ground white pepper
chopped parsley, to garnish

A variation of the classic French dish, coq au vin, this German version tastes quite different because the chicken is cooked in a German white wine, not red as in the original French recipe.

Duck Legs with Red Cabbage
Knusprige Entenkeule mit Rotkohl

Serves 4

8 duck legs or 4 goose legs
10ml/2 tsp tomato purée (paste)
200l/7fl oz/scant 1 cup red wine
salt and ground white pepper
chopped parsley, to garnish
potato dumplings, to serve

For the red cabbage

3 onions
60g/2½oz lard
1 red cabbage, quartered, cored and
   finely sliced
100ml/3½fl oz/½ cup red wine
   vinegar
15ml/1 tbsp sugar
2 bay leaves
3 pieces star anise
1 cinnamon stick
200ml/7fl oz/scant 1 cup apple juice
2 apples, chopped
30ml/2 tbsp redcurrant jelly
5ml/1 tsp cornflour (cornstarch)

1 To make the cabbage, chop two of the onions, melt the lard in a pan and fry the onion for 2 minutes. Add the cabbage, vinegar, sugar, spices and apple juice, bring to the boil, cover and simmer for 30 minutes.

2 Preheat the oven to 200°C/400°F/Gas 6. Stir in the apples and redcurrant jelly and cook for a further 45 minutes, adding more apple juice if necessary. Towards the end of the cooking time, blend the cornflour with water and stir into the cabbage.

3 While the cabbage is cooking, place the duck legs in a roasting tin (pan), season, add a cup of water and roast in the oven for 20 minutes, then reduce the temperature to 160°C/325°F/Gas 3 and cook for a further 40 minutes, basting from time to time.

4 When the legs are cooked, lift them out and keep them warm. Add the remaining onion, chopped, and the tomato purée to the pan and fry over high heat for 3–4 minutes. Deglaze the pan with the wine and cook for another 2 minutes. Serve the duck legs with the sauce poured over, garnished with parsley and accompanied by the red cabbage. Serve with potato dumplings.

COOK'S TIP

To make the potato dumplings, mix 1kg/2lb mashed potato with 150g/5oz plain (all-purpose) flour and form into balls. Drop into boiling salted water, allow them to rise to the surface and cook for 5 minutes.

This is another Christmas dish, traditionally served with potato dumplings. Germans will usually use goose legs rather than duck legs, but if goose is not available, duck legs have the same rich texture and flavour.

Venison Goulash with Potato Cakes
Hirschgoulasch mit Kartoffelplätzchen

Serves 4

800g/1¾lb boneless venison, cubed
3 bay leaves
5 juniper berries, crushed
1 cinnamon stick
sunflower oil, for frying
2 onions, chopped
10ml/2 tsp tomato purée (paste)
300ml/½ pint/1¼ cups red wine
1 litre/2¾ pints/4 cups chicken stock
250g/9oz brown cap (cremini)
    mushrooms, quartered
15ml/1 tbsp sour cream
200ml/7fl oz/scant 1 cup gin
oil, for frying
salt and ground white pepper

For the potato cakes

500g1¼lb floury potatoes, peeled
3 egg yolks
15ml/1 tbsp flour
50g/2oz/4 tbsp butter
sunflower oil, for frying
salt and freshly grated nutmeg
small bunch chives, chopped

1 Rub the meat with the spices and some oil and leave overnight. Next day, heat 3–4 tbsp oil in a large pan over high heat and fry the venison for 5–6 minutes on each side.

2 Add the chopped onion and cook for another 4–5 minutes. Add the tomato purée, red wine and the stock to the pan and bring to the boil. Reduce the heat and simmer for 40 minutes or until the meat is tender, adding more stock if necessary. Add the mushrooms and cook for a further 20 minutes.

3 Meanwhile, boil the potatoes in salted water until tender, then drain and mash. Beat in the egg yolks, flour, butter and chives and season with salt and nutmeg. When cool enough to handle, form into 8–10 cakes. Heat a little oil in a large frying pan and fry the cakes for 2–3 minutes on each side.

4 Just before serving, stir the sour cream and gin into the venison goulash. Serve immediately with the hot, golden brown potato cakes.

The dark red meat and strong smell and taste of venison is very distinctive. Germany is heavily forested, so venison, wild boar and hare are on the menu throughout the country. This rich goulash is marinated overnight to add extra flavour. It is traditionally served with potato cakes.

Bavarian Cream with Berries
Bayrisch Creme mit Beeren

Serves 4

300ml/½ pint/1¼ cups milk
1 vanilla pod (bean)
4 egg yolks
150g/5oz/1¼ cups caster (superfine)
    sugar
7 gelatine leaves, soaked in water for
    10 minutes
10ml/2 tsp almond liqueur
300ml/½ pint/1¼ cups double
    (heavy) cream, whipped until stiff
mint leaves, to decorate
compote of berries or fresh
    strawberries, to serve
    (see opposite)

1 Put the milk in a pan. Cut the vanilla pod in half lengthways and scrape out the seeds. Add the pod and the seeds to the milk and heat to boiling point, then remove the pan from the heat.

2 Whisk the egg yolks with the sugar until light and thick, then whisk in the hot milk (discard the vanilla pod). Set the bowl over a pan of simmering water and heat the mixture very slowly, stirring, until it thickens. Remove the pan from the heat.

3 Take the gelatine leaves out of the water and squeeze out any excess. Place the leaves in a pan with the liqueur and heat until melted, then stir this mixture into the custard. Fold the whipped cream into the custard.

4 Divide the mixture among four serving bowls and chill for 3 hours until set. Serve with a compote of cherries, or fresh strawberries, decorated with mint leaves.

Every apprentice German chef has to learn this classic recipe. A soft, sweet cream with the unique aroma of fresh vanilla, served with a compote of cherries or strawberries, it makes a delightful end to a meal.

Red Fruit Compote Hamburg-style
Hamburger Rote Grütze

Serves 4

20g/¾oz caster (superfine) sugar
200ml/7fl oz/scant 1 cup red grape
   juice
2 pieces of star anise
1 cinnamon stick
15g/½oz/2 tbsp cornflour
   (cornstarch)
450g/1lb mixed berries (strawberries,
   blueberries, cranberries,
   blackberries, raspberries or
   redcurrants), washed
fresh mint leaves, to decorate
single (light) cream, to serve

*A wonderful and simple
dessert. During the summer
it can be made with fresh
berries, but you can also
use frozen fruit. Though it
comes from the northern
region, this well-known
compote is eaten all
over Germany.*

1 Heat the sugar in a pan over medium heat until it caramelizes. When it turns golden brown, plunge the base of the pan in a bowl of cold water to stop the sugar burning. Stir in the grape juice, add the spices and return to the heat.

2 Mix the cornflour with a little cold water. When the juice comes to the boil, stir in the cornflour mixture and cook, stirring, for 1 minute to thicken.

3 Halve any large berries, and add them all to the hot juice, bring to the boil again, then remove from the heat and leave to cool. Spoon the cold compote into bowls, decorate with mint leaves and serve with cream.

Apple Fritters with Fruits in Rum
Apfelkrapfen mit Rumtopf

Serves 4

200g/7oz/1¾ cups self-raising
   (self-rising) flour
100ml/3½ fl oz/scant ½ cup milk
5ml/1 tsp baking powder
40g/1oz caster (superfine) sugar
pinch of salt
5ml/1 tsp butter
2 apples
sunflower oil, for deep-frying
icing (confectioners') sugar, to dust
Rumtopf, to serve

1 Mix the flour and milk in a bowl and add the baking powder, sugar and salt. Melt the butter in a small pan until it starts to brown, then mix it into the batter.

2 Heat the oil in a deep-fryer to 180°C/350°F. Peel and core the apples and cut them into thick rings. Dip them in the batter, making sure that they are completely covered, then drop them straight into the hot oil and deep-fry for 2–3 minutes, until the batter is crisp and golden brown.

3 Drain the fritters on kitchen paper, dust with icing sugar and serve immediately with a spoonful of fruit from the Rumtopf.

VARIATION

If you don't have any Rumtopf, lightly poach a mixture of berries with sugar, rum and water, to make a quick version of a compote.

*Fruit fritters are a very popular dessert in Germany.
At festivals you can smell them cooking from far off,
and the aroma draws you like a magnet. Here, they are
served with Rumtopf, a delicious traditional German
preserve made by preserving fresh fruit in sugar
and rum in a large jar called a rum pot.*

Apple Strudel Apfelstrudel

1 Mix the flour with the oil and water to make a smooth dough. Put it in an oiled bowl, cover and leave for 30 minutes in a warm place.

2 To make the filling, soak the raisins in the brandy for 20 minutes. Slice the apples thinly, put them in a bowl and mix with the lemon juice. Add the vanilla sugar, sugar, chopped hazelnuts and breadcrumbs.

3 Preheat the oven to 160°C/325°F/Gas 3. Spread a clean dish towel on the work surface and dust it with flour. Roll out the dough on the towel, then stretch it carefully on all sides using your hands, until it is the same size as the cloth. It should now be very thin.

4 Spoon the apple filling along the lower part of the dough, leaving a space of 4cm/1½in on each side. Brush all the edges with melted butter. Turn in the sides of the dough, then use the towel to help you roll up the strudel around the filling. Brush with the rest of the melted butter and transfer it carefully to a baking tray lined with baking parchment.

5 Bake for 20–30 minutes, until the pastry is golden brown and crisp. Remove the strudel from the oven and leave it to cool for a few minutes.

6 To make the sauce, cut the vanilla pod in half lengthways and scrape out the seeds. Put the milk and cream in a pan with the vanilla pod and seeds. Heat to boiling point, then remove from the heat. Whisk the egg yolks with the sugar until light and thick, then whisk in the hot milk (having removed the vanilla pod). Set the bowl over a pan of simmering water and heat the sauce gently, stirring constantly, until it thickens. Dust the strudel with sugar, slice and serve warm with the vanilla sauce.

Originally from Austria, this dessert quickly became a classic in Germany too. The difficult part is stretching the strudel dough until it is really thin: my first head chef told me that you should be able to read a newspaper through it.

Serves 4

100g/3½oz strong white (bread) flour, plus extra for dusting
5ml/1 tsp sunflower oil
30–35ml/6–7 tsp lukewarm water
50g/2oz/4 tbsp butter, melted
icing (confectioners') sugar, to dust

For the filling

10ml/2 tsp raisins
10ml/2 tsp brandy
400g/14oz apples, peeled and cored
juice of 1 lemon
5ml/1 tsp vanilla sugar or 2.5ml/½ tsp vanilla extract
100g/3½oz caster (superfine) sugar
25g/1oz/¼ cup hazelnuts, finely chopped
50g/2oz/1 cup fresh breadcrumbs

For the vanilla sauce

1 vanilla pod (bean)
200ml/7fl oz/scant 1 cup milk
100ml/3½fl oz/scant ½ cup single (light) cream
3 egg yolks
25g/1oz caster (superfine) sugar, or to taste

Black Forest Gateau Schwarzwälder Kirschtorte

Makes about 12 slices

100g/3½oz plain (bittersweet)
chocolate

100g/3½oz/7 tbsp butter, softened

100g/3½oz/½ cup caster (superfine)
sugar

2 tsp vanilla extract or 3 packs vanilla
sugar (about 20g/¾oz)

6 eggs, separated

pinch of salt

100g/3½oz plain (all-purpose) flour

50g/2oz/½ cup cornflour (cornstarch)

5ml/1 tsp baking powder

For the filling

500g/1¼ lb bottled cherries

5 gelatine leaves, soaked in cold
water for 5 minutes

750ml/1¼ pints/3 cups double
(heavy) cream

5ml/1 tsp vanilla extract or 1 pack
vanilla sugar (about 5g/2.5ml)

100ml/3½fl oz/scant ½ cup Kirsch

To decorate

12 glacé (candied) cherries

75g/3oz flaked chocolate

1 Break up the chocolate and melt it in a bowl over a pan of gently simmering water. Preheat the oven to 160°C/325°F/Gas 3. Butter a 30cm/12in cake tin (pan).

2 Cream the butter with the sugar and vanilla extract or sugar. Gradually beat in the egg yolks, until the mixture is light and foamy. Mix in the melted chocolate. Beat the egg whites with a pinch of salt until stiff and fold them into the mixture. Sift the flour with the baking powder and fold in. Turn the mixture into the prepared tin and bake for 45–60 minutes, until a skewer pushed into the centre comes out clean. Leave to cool a little in the tin, then take out and leave on a rack to cool completely.

3 Strain the juice off the cherries, reserving the fruit, and put it in a pan. Bring to the boil, remove from the heat and add the gelatine leaves. Stir until the gelatine has dissolved, then leave to cool. Whip the cream with the vanilla until stiff.

4 Slice the cake into three layers. Sprinkle the bottom layer with half the Kirsch, then spread some of the cherry jelly over it and put half the cherries on top. Top with some cream. Put the second layer of cake on top, and repeat the layers of Kirsch, jelly, cherries and cream. Top with the final cake layer.

5 Spread cream around the sides of the cake, and pipe 12 whirls on the top, adding a glacé cherry to each. Sprinkle some of the flaked chocolate on top of the cake and press the rest into the sides. Chill for 4–5 hours before serving.

Famous all over the world, this is the archetypal German cake. The name explains its origin, but it is eaten all over Germany. It's laden with calories, but don't think about that while you're eating it, just enjoy it!

Makes 3 cakes

500g/1¼lb/3½ cups sultanas (golden raisins)
100ml/3½fl oz/scant ½ cup brandy
500ml/17fl oz/generous 2 cups milk
75g/3oz fresh yeast
1kg/2¼lb plain (all-purpose) flour
150g/5oz/¾ cup caster (superfine) sugar
10ml/2 tsp vanilla extract or 3 packs vanilla sugar (about 20g/¾oz)
generous pinch of salt
generous pinch each ground cardamom, cinnamon and ginger
500g/1¼lb/2½ cups butter, plus extra for brushing
150g/5oz/1¼ cups chopped almonds
150g/5oz marzipan, chopped
100g/3½oz/⅔ cup candied lemon peel
100g/3½oz/⅔ cup candied orange peel
icing (confectioners') sugar, to dust

Stollen Stollen

1 Soak the sultanas in the brandy for 3–4 hours. Preheat the oven to 160°C/325°F/Gas 3.

2 Heat the milk to about 50°C/120°F, add the yeast and stir until it has dissolved. Put the flour and sugar into a large bowl, make a well in the centre and pour in the milk. Draw in the dry ingredients and knead with both hands until you have a smooth dough. Leave to rest in a warm place for 1 hour.

3 Add the vanilla, salt, spices and the butter, cut into small pieces, and knead the dough again for 3–5 minutes.

4 Add the chopped almonds and the marzipan to the bowl and knead thoroughly into the dough. Then add the candied peel and the sultanas and knead again for at least 3 minutes.

5 Divide the dough into three equal pieces, and form each into a long shape with rounded ends. Line a baking sheet with baking parchment and lay the three stollen on it. Bake for 45–60 minutes, until risen and golden brown.

6 Melt some butter in a pan and brush it over the warm stollen, then dust them thickly with icing sugar and leave to cool.

COOK'S TIP

Stollen is usually made in a large batch, as here, to last over the winter months. It will keep well if wrapped up tightly and stored in a dry place.

This delicious cake, with its luxurious filling, is eaten in the period before Christmas. The recipe comes from Dresden, and only cakes made in this region can be given the name 'Christstollen'.

Gingerbread Lebkuchen

Makes 30 squares

300g/11oz/scant 3 cups hazelnuts,
  skinned
300g/11oz/1½ cups soft brown
  sugar
5 eggs
150g/5oz/10 tbsp butter, melted
100g/3½oz/½ cup honey
500g/1¼lb/5 cups plain (all-purpose)
  flour
25ml/5 tsp baking powder
25g/1oz Lebkuchen spice mix

Gingerbread belongs to Christmas just as much as presents under the Christmas tree. It is flavoured with cloves, cinnamon, ginger, cardamom, allspice and nutmeg, which can now be bought as Lebkuchen mix.

1 Preheat the oven to 160°C/325°F/Gas 3 and line a 40x30cm/16x12in baking tray with baking parchment.

2 Heat a frying pan over medium heat and toast the hazelnuts, moving them around so that they brown evenly. Remove from the heat, cool, then chop finely.

3 Beat the sugar with the eggs until the mixture is light and thick. Stir in the melted butter, the honey and the chopped hazelnuts. Sift the flour with the baking powder and spice mix and fold into the mixture.

4 Pour the batter into the prepared tray. Bake in the preheated oven for about 45 minutes. Take it out and leave to cool in the tin before cutting into squares.

Nutritional notes

Parsnip Soup with Black Forest Ham: Energy 304kcal/1266kJ; Protein 12g; Carbohydrate 17.8g, of which sugars 10.6g; Fat 21g, of which saturates 11.1g; Cholesterol 73mg; Calcium 77mg; Fibre 4.8g; Sodium 718mg

Carrot and Apple Cream Soup: Energy 341kcal/1412kJ; Protein 3g; Carbohydrate 18.2g, of which sugars 16.5g; Fat 27.2g, of which saturates 16.8g; Cholesterol 71mg; Calcium 84mg; Fibre 3.7g; Sodium 150mg

Asparagus and Smoked Fish Salad: Energy 644kcal/2664kJ; Protein 34.2g; Carbohydrate 13.4g, of which sugars 12.5g; Fat 50.9g, of which saturates 14.4g; Cholesterol 230mg; Calcium 319mg; Fibre 6.1g; Sodium 864mg

Tartare of Matjes Herring and Salmon: Energy 255kcal/1057kJ; Protein 18.1g; Carbohydrate 4g, of which sugars 3.3g; Fat 15.9g, of which saturates 4.4g; Cholesterol 62mg; Calcium 41mg; Fibre 0.7g; Sodium 85mg

Potato Salad with Frankfurters: Energy 536kcal/2234kJ; Protein 22.2g; Carbohydrate 42.5g, of which sugars 11g; Fat 31.9g, of which saturates 10.8g; Cholesterol 85mg; Calcium 66mg; Fibre 4g; Sodium 1276mg

Red Cabbage Salad with Walnuts: Energy 240kcal/991kJ; Protein 5.6g; Carbohydrate 12.4g, of which sugars 12.1g; Fat 18.8g, of which saturates 1.7g; Cholesterol 0mg; Calcium 116mg; Fibre 4.9g; Sodium 16mg

Spätzle with Cheese and Onions: Energy 900kcal/3778kJ; Protein 41.4g; Carbohydrate 111.5g, of which sugars 13.3g; Fat 34.8g, of which saturates 16.6g; Cholesterol 350mg; Calcium 818mg; Fibre 6.3g; Sodium 832mg

Potato Pancakes with Smoked Salmon: Energy 711kcal/2982kJ; Protein 37.5g; Carbohydrate 76.9g, of which sugars 16g; Fat 30.4g, of which saturates 11.1g; Cholesterol 224mg; Calcium 185mg; Fibre 6.6g; Sodium 1773mg

Nuremberg Sausages with Apple Sauerkraut: Energy 644kcal/2675kJ; Protein 18.6g; Carbohydrate 34g, of which sugars 17.5g; Fat 49.1g, of which saturates 19.8g; Cholesterol 81mg; Calcium 159mg; Fibre 5.2g; Sodium 2207mg

Apple and Potato Mash with Black Pudding: Energy 855kcal/3559kJ; Protein 20.8g; Carbohydrate 61g, of which sugars 19.7g; Fat 60.4g, of which saturates 26.7g; Cholesterol 156mg; Calcium 193mg; Fibre 4.9g; Sodium 1767mg

Matjes Herring with Bacon and Onions: Energy 970kcal/4032kJ; Protein 47.4g; Carbohydrate 58.1g, of which sugars 16g; Fat 53.4g, of which saturates 26.1g; Cholesterol 203mg; Calcium 199mg; Fibre 9.8g; Sodium 1103mg

Fish Fillets in Creamy Mustard Sauce: Energy 570kcal/2387kJ; Protein 47.9g; Carbohydrate 42.5g, of which sugars 5.1g; Fat 24.1g, of which saturates 6.9g; Cholesterol 126mg; Calcium 62mg; Fibre 2.7g; Sodium 738mg

Rhenish Mussels with Root Vegetables: Energy 278kcal/1169kJ; Protein 28g; Carbohydrate 16.8g, of which sugars 14.5g; Fat 6.4g, of which saturates 0.9g; Cholesterol 60mg; Calcium 376mg; Fibre 4.1g; Sodium 371mg

Simmered Beef Topside with Horseradish: Energy 653kcal/2747kJ; Protein 65g; Carbohydrate 44.3g, of which sugars 26g; Fat 25.3g, of which saturates 13g; Cholesterol 171mg; Calcium 281.5mg; Fibre 10.8g; Sodium 576mg

Veal Meatballs in White Caper Sauce: Energy 722kcal/3018kJ; Protein 59.9g; Carbohydrate 30.1g, of which sugars 7.2g; Fat 41.2g, of which saturates 20.9g; Cholesterol 306mg; Calcium 160mg; Fibre 2g; Sodium 554mg

Cabbage Stuffed with Pork: Energy 683kcal/2847kJ; Protein 54g; Carbohydrate 23.2g, of which sugars 8.7g; Fat 42.4g, of which saturates 12.4g; Cholesterol 254mg; Calcium 110mg; Fibre 2.8g; Sodium 1074mg

Chicken in Riesling with Roast Potatoes: Energy 1416kcal/5881kJ; Protein 63.4g; Carbohydrate 49.9g, of which sugars 20.2g; Fat 103.9g, of which saturates 52.1g; Cholesterol 414mg; Calcium 386mg; Fibre 2.6g; Sodium 414mg

Duck Legs with Red Cabbage: Energy 958kcal/3961kJ; Protein 20.7g; Carbohydrate 32.7g, of which sugars 28.5g; Fat 79.8g, of which saturates 22.8g; Cholesterol 12mg; Calcium 122mg; Fibre 5.1g; Sodium 146mg

Venison Goulash with Potato Cakes: Energy 618kcal/2591kJ; Protein 4g; Carbohydrate 8g, of which sugars 7.1g; Fat 20g, of which saturates 5.7g; Cholesterol 4mg; Calcium 30.5mg; Fibre 1.5g; Sodium 36.5mg

Bavarian Cream with Berries: Energy 587kcal/2443kJ; Protein 6.8g; Carbohydrate 45.8g, of which sugars 45.8g; Fat 47.1g, of which saturates 24.8g; Cholesterol 304mg; Calcium 171mg; Fibre 0g; Sodium 81mg

Red Fruit Jelly Hamburg-style: Energy 86kcal/366kJ; Protein 1.1g; Carbohydrate 21.3g, of which sugars 17.8g; Fat 0.2g, of which saturates 0g; Cholesterol 0mg; Calcium 31mg; Fibre 1.3g; Sodium 13mg

Apple Fritters with Fruits in Rum: Energy 391kcal/1644kJ; Protein 5.5g; Carbohydrate 54g, of which sugars 16.8g; Fat 18.6g, of which saturates 2.8g; Cholesterol 4mg; Calcium 213mg; Fibre 2.4g; Sodium 205mg

Apple Strudel: Energy 525kcal/2207kJ; Protein 8.9g; Carbohydrate 69.6g, of which sugars 41g; Fat 24.9g, of which saturates 11.6g; Cholesterol 195mg; Calcium 151mg; Fibre 3.1g; Sodium 228mg

Black Forest Gateau: Energy 551kcal/2293kJ; Protein 5.7g; Carbohydrate 36.8g, of which sugars 26.2g; Fat 45.7g, of which saturates 25.5g; Cholesterol 196mg; Calcium 73mg; Fibre 0.5g; Sodium 128mg

Stollen: Energy 3829kcal/16069kJ; Protein 55.8g; Carbohydrate 511.9g, of which sugars 256.5g; Fat 178.8g, of which saturates 95.3g; Cholesterol 393mg; Calcium 1065mg; Fibre 21.5g; Sodium 1590mg

Gingerbread: Energy 741kcal/3106kJ; Protein 14.1g; Carbohydrate 89.1g, of which sugars 45.4g; Fat 38.9g, of which saturates 11.5g; Cholesterol 144mg; Calcium 166mg; Fibre 3.8g; Sodium 171mg

Index